Johnson,

The Men of MARCH

And

60 Inspiring Quotes to Live By

Milford Johnson

Papyrus Publishing Inc.

© 2023 Milford Johnson

First Printing

Printed in the United States of America.

Milford Johnson, the Men of MARCH
and 60 Inspiring Quotes to Live By
by Milford Johnson

ISBN 978-0-9882883-4-8 Softcover

Summary:
This book documents the life and work of Elder Milford Johnson who was the host and producer of Senior Perspectives, a public affairs show on KMOJ 89.9 FM for over 20 years from 2000 - 2022. He is a member of MARCH (Men Are Responsible for Cultivating Hope) also known as the Men of MARCH since 1995.

Publications Team:
Nathaniel Khaliq, Alemu Foluke, Akil Foluke, Tyrone Terrill
Proofreading — Uri-Biia Si-Asar
Book Design —Papyrus Publishing Inc.
Printer — Bookmobile, Minneapolis, MN

Photo Credits:
Milford Johnson, *In Black Ink*
1994 MARCH members, *Gene McMillen*
Million Man March on the Washington Plaza
    Nation of Islam
March members throughout the years
    Tyrone Terrill Photo Collection
Washington Mall at the Million Man March
    Library of Congress, Washington, D.C.
    (reproduction no. LC-DIG-ppmsca-38892)

Papyrus Publishing Inc.
7409 Edgewood Avenue North
Brooklyn Park, MN 55428
PapyrusPublishing@msn.com

PAPYRUS
PUBLISHING

Dedication

To my wife of over fifty years…
Lois Kinny

To my daughter Charlotte Lucille Johnson, who is the sweetest and cutest woman you'd ever want to see. She is a real warrior, a great soldier, and at the age of 67, she has never let epilepsy bother her.

Milford Johnson

"I am ONE in a Million!"

Long Live the Spirit of the
Million Man March.

Men Are Responsible for Cultivating Hope
(MARCH)

Contents

My Story

I was born in September of 1932 in Wichita, Kansas. I went to an all-Black elementary and junior high school. I attended East High, an integrated high school. My mother, Alice Johnson, raised me and taught me manners, respect, dependability, and honesty. She was very religious. She didn't even allow pork chops in the house. As a matter of fact that's what got my father in big trouble when he cooked some in the house one day. I was raised near the railroad tracks where the Black community was on the westside of Wichita. In my neighborhood, I grew up with fifteen guys and sixteen gals. They were like my extended family. We did everything together. One thing I remember my mother telling me was, "Don't go down a road that you can't come back on." My mother didn't read when I was a child. However, this brilliant woman learned to read with me when she put me in school. Every reading lesson and homework assignment I had, she would help me with, and we would learn together. This process happened over years. She became an avid reader. Her favorite book was the Bible, which she read every day.

My father was a different story. I wasn't raised by my father really. From the age of eight to sixteen years old, I shined shoes at the neighborhood barbershop. This barbershop was run by Mr. Taban, Mr. Henry, and Mr. Folks. In fact, they raised me to the extent that they could and somewhat taught me to be a man. They would take me out to lunch all the time and tell me about life, women, dating, relationships, and manhood. I will never forget their guidance, mentorship, and modeling of Black manhood.

I quit school in the 11th grade because Wichita was a very prejudice and racist town. White kids were very mean to us. They thought that East High School was their school and Negroes weren't supposed to be there. Many won't believe this, but I grew up celebrating Negro History Week which was created by Dr. Carter G. Woodson. It was one of the things I enjoyed about school. Today it is called Black History Month. In 11th grade, I took an American History class but it was all about white people, their life, and their accomplishments. I knew about famous Black people like Dr. George Washington Carver, Marion Anderson, and the Brown Bomber Joe Louis, the heavyweight champion of the world. I knew we had great Black

people but they weren't recognized or taught in school.

One year, I couldn't wait for Negro History Week. On the first day of Negro History Week, my American History teacher said that we were going to learn about Negroes during this week. My chest stuck out and I was proud. So she said to turn to a particular page in our textbooks. I was so excited that we were going to learn about me and my people. I turned to the page and there were only two pages about Negroes in that 500-page book. On that page was information about John Brown, a white abolitionist. He was a great man and I admired him. John Brown's family was killed fighting against slavery. However, I wanted these white students to see and hear about great Black people. Since that didn't happen, I slammed my book shut, got up, and walked home. That was my last day of high school.

On my way home, I walked by a Selective Service Office that enlisted people in the military. I asked the lady there if I could sign up and she said yes. At that time, they needed everyone they could get to fight in the Korean War. So in 1956 when I was seventeen years old, I ended up in the Air Force. I

became a demolition expert. My experience in the military taught me structure, respect, and precision. It also reinforced in me how to be timely and efficient. Even how to make my bed the military way, which my mother had already taught me.

When I came back from the service after four years, I went to barbering school in Kansas City, Missouri. I reconnected with a girl that I went to school with since the 6th grade. Her name was Lois Kinny, and she had always said that I was her boyfriend. Well, I married her and had three children. I bought a house that I own to this day. Well, I married her and I bought a house in an all-white neighborhood in Wichita, Kansas. I rented it out to a colonel from the nearby Air Force Base. I rented the house to him for three times my monthly mortgage for about three years. During this time, my wife and I stayed in a low-rent basement apartment. We had three children - my daughter, the oldest, Charlotte, then my son Michael, and my youngest son, Tony. I still own this house today.

I rented a barber's chair from a local barbershop owned by Bill Wigley. Bill and I became best of friends. He was my main man and we hung out together all the time. I was a very popular barber in

the 60s when the afros were out. I barbered from 1958 through 1969. During that time, I went to Wichita State and earned my Communications degree. I also obtained my FCC Broadcasting license. I had several shows regarding Black affairs and issues in Wichita for several years.

In the 1960s, I joined the Black Power movement and became a Black Panther in Wichita. I met Malcolm X in the early 60s when I traveled to New York and he affectionately called me "Wichita!" I was going to join the Nation of Islam, but that never happened because Malcolm was assassinated. While studying with Malcolm X, he taught me about the five daily prayers from the Quran. I say these same prayers today. In Wichita, I came under some political heat due to my involvement in our freedom movement and had to leave. So I came to Saint Paul, Minnesota in 1969. I came to Minnesota because my good friend also from Wichita was there. Thomas Muata Ross my brother-in-spirit (may he rest in peace) relocated years before me to Minnesota with his sister and he said Minneapolis and Saint Paul were good places with many opportunities for Brothers like myself.

When I arrived in Minnesota, I connected with Brothers like David Pettiford and Kelly Daye and continued activism in our movement. One day in 1967, I was at a march/protest on Plymouth Avenue North and a young man gave me a paper with some information on it. This young man was none other than Dr. Mahmoud El-Kati and he was the Director of Education at The Way Opportunities Inc. The paper had a quote on it by Frederick Douglass from 1884 where he wrote in a private letter, "I am for any movement where there is a just cause to promote, a right to be asserted, a chain to be broken, a burden to be lifted, and a wrong to be redressed. In the struggle for Social Justice, the only reward is to be in the struggle." I read this quote every day and I read it on my weekly radio show on KMOJ. Along with Mahmoud, I met Spike Moss who was a youth leader of The Way at the time.

During the 1970s in Saint Paul, I was a bus driver and worked for the Metropolitan Transit Company (MTC) for twenty-five years. I worked in a group home at 715 Dayton Avenue. This group home helped many young Black men get on their feet and stay out of jail. These men were placed in the home by the courts. Not too far from the group home on the corner of Selby and Grotto, there was business

or factory there called Control Data. It was Black ran and operated twenty-four hours a day. I had never seen that before and never seen that after. Black people hiring all these Black people from their own community. Dick Mangrum was the Executive Director of this wonderful venture.

I am a member of the NAACP, and I was involved in the Urban League in Saint Paul (before it closed) and Minneapolis. I was involved in the African American Leadership Council in Saint Paul and the African American Leadership Forum in Minneapolis. I was a volunteer at the Council on Black Minnesotans, a statewide agency too.

In 1994, Malcolm X's daughter Qubilah Shabazz came to Minnesota to live with her teen son. Apparently, she had some problems with the government criminal justice system as she was accused of trying to hire a hitman to kill the Nation of Islam leader Minister Louis Farrakhan. The background for this charge comes from the 60s, when several men from the Nation of Islam murdered Malcolm X and there was controversy on whether Louis Farrakhan help create the atmosphere for that evil act to occur. The government tried to build a case of Malcolm X's

daughter seeking revenge for her father's death. Most in the Black community thought these were trumped up charges. There was an announcement that Black men would go to the court house to support her. Since I was a follower of Malcolm X, I had to get involved. Qubilah was the second of six daughters born to Malcolm X and Betty Shabazz. When I went to the court house I met some very powerful men like Tyrone Terrill and Keith Ellison. It turned out Qubilah was found innocent of the charges. However, I stayed connected with the men I met there at the courthouse.

These same men were organizing for the Million Man March that was held October 16th, 1995. Randy Staten, Minister James Muhammad, Tyrone Terrill, Keith Ellison, Mahmoud El-Kati, Kamau Kambui, myself, and others went to the Million Man March in Washington, DC. I remember from the trip that we had a meeting the night before the March and I met a young man named James Sanderson, who was part of a group called Salaam. We became best friends. I also became a member of MARCH, an organization that we started after we returned from the Million Man March. Men Are Responsible for Cultivating Hope (MARCH) is an organization of Black men and boys learning

together, supporting one another, and serving the community. At the Million Man March, Minister Farrakhan had the million plus men take an oath to go back to our communities and build them, protect them, and fight for them. Thomas Muata Ross was a great little brother of mine. Muata and I taught young Brothers for twenty years at Harvest Preparatory School in North Minneapolis about their history, heritage, and culture. We essentially had a Rites of Passage program. MARCH was always intergenerational. Young Brothers or the Junior men of MARCH learned about the US Constitution and the Thirteenth, Fourteenth, and Fifteenth Amendments. MARCH would marshal various community events such as the annual Dr. Martin Luther King Jr. Celebration and Rondo Days in Saint Paul, Minnesota. I will share more about this organization in the coming pages in hope that others will continue on this great work in our community, whether with MARCH or with another organization. The principles and strategies for struggle embodied in MARCH are universal for Black people and can be applied personally and collectively.

In 2000, I was given the opportunity to start my own radio show for seniors living in public housing

and around the metro area. Ms. Cora McCorvey, former Executive Director/CEO of the Minneapolis Public Housing Authority (MPHA) was instrumental in making this program happen. My one-hour show ran for over twenty years every Saturday morning from 8:00 a.m. – 9:00 a.m. on KMOJ FM 89.9 radio station in North Minneapolis. My main man Q-Bear, KMOJ's program director, provided me with production support for my show. I'm grateful to him and KMOJ for all their support over these years.

In 2022, at the age of eighty-nine, my sons, Tony Johnson and Chad Bell, came up to help me pack and take me back home to Witchita, Kansas. I returned home to my family in Wichita, Kansas to be with my children: Charlotte, Michael, Tony, Chad, and my many grandchildren. I will miss Minneapolis and Saint Paul, and all the friends and community members that showed me love, support, and brotherhood. Hotep (Peace).

Mission and Purpose of MARCH

MARCH is an organization comprised of Black men whose primary purpose is to liberate and free the Black man, woman, and child. We repudiate any and all who would utilize gender as a means of causing friction or disunity between our men and women. Our respect for our women is total and complete. We do realize there is much that Black men need to do, and we have committed ourselves to doing it. We are committed to the social, political, religious, and economic empowerment of Black people at every level of our community. All Black men are welcome to join regardless of religion, economic status, political, or social circumstances. MARCH stands in complete solidarity with all people who seek freedom, justice, and equity and are committed to unity in the Black community.

The Million Man March Pledge

The pledge that Minister Louis Farrakhan asked Black men to take on October 16, 1995, during the Million Man March on Washington, D.C.

I PLEDGE that from this day forward I will strive to love my brother as I love myself. I, from this day forward, will strive to improve myself spiritually, morally, mentally, socially, politically, and economically for the benefit of myself, my family, and my people. I pledge that I will strive to build businesses, build houses, build hospitals, build factories, and enter into international trade for the good of myself, my family, and my people.

I PLEDGE that from this day forward I will never raise my hand with a knife or a gun to beat, cut, or shoot any member of my family or any human being except in self-defense. I pledge from this day forward I will never abuse my wife by striking her, disrespecting her, for she is the mother of my children and the producer of my future. I pledge that from this

day forward I will never engage in the abuse of children, little boys or little girls for sexual gratification. For I will let them grow in peace to be strong men and women for the future of our people.

I WILL never again use the 'B word' to describe any female. But particularly my own Black sister. I pledge from this day forward that I will not poison my body with drugs or that which is destructive to my health and my well-being. I pledge from this day forward I will support Black newspapers, Black radio, and Black television. I will support Black artists who clean up their acts to show respect for themselves and respect for their people and respect for the ears of the human family. I will do all of this so help me God.

Eight Steps of Atonement

During Minister Farrakhan's address at The Million Man March, he outlined Eight Principled Steps in the Atonement Process. Atonement is a process of moving oneself and/or group from injustice to justice, from imbalance to balance, from wrong to right, from sickness to health, or from complacency to transformation. Simply stated, they are as follows:

1. Point out the wrong

Whether the wrong is pointed out by you or others, there can be sad and rejected feelings with this discovery. However, we must humbly accept the truth and move on with the atonement process.

2. Acknowledge

Admit the existence of the alleged wrong: being in a state of recognition of the truth and the fact that we have been wronged or committed a wrong.

3. Confess

Only true confession can grant us protection from the wrong and prepare us for reconciliation.

4. Repentance

Without repentance, we will keep doing the wrong over and over.

5. Atonement

To make amends or reparations, is to do something about what is going on in our lives, the lives of our family members, and in the African American community.

6. Forgiveness

Pardon for or remission of: to absolve, to clear, to exonerate and liberate, cease negative feelings and resentment toward another.

7. Reconciliation & Restoration

To reconcile and restore, becoming peaceful and friendly to settle what made the division.

8. Union with the Creator

A perfect union, at peace with the Creator. Only the Creator can liberate the soul from sin.

The Black Agenda
The Issues of The Millions More Movement
October 15, 2005

1. Unity

We call, first, for unity amongst Black peoples and organizations. We call for unity amongst all African people and people of African descent worldwide. We call for unity with our Brown, Red, disenfranchised, and oppressed brothers and sisters in America, the Caribbean, Central and South America, Asia, and all over the world. "The Power of One" is the synthesis of men, women, youth, and elders working in unity for our total liberation.

2. Spiritual Values

We call for atonement, reconciliation, and responsibility. We organize in the name of our God (The One Creator) and on sound ethics, moral principles, and values. Our movement affirms the rich legacy and diversity of our spiritual traditions and calls for unity and understanding among our religious faiths and spiritual traditions.

3. Education

We demand an end to substandard education in our community. The Millions More Movement advocates and will develop a new independent educational paradigm for our people. We must have a knowledge of self, our history, and the best education in civilized society. We will build a skills bank with talent that will be used in the development of our people.

Below are excerpts from the Final Call's interview with Dr. Maulana Karenga on his comments on the educational component of the Million Man March 1995/Millions More Movement's 2006 Action Agenda.

> We must wage a two-track and simultaneous struggle for quality education in the Black community. First, we must continue and expand support for African-centered independent schools through joining their boards, enrolling our children, being concerned and active parents, donating time, services and monies to them, and working in various other ways to insure that they provide the highest level of culturally-rooted education, as well as academic excellence and social responsibility.

Secondly, we must intensify and broaden the struggle for quality public education through heightened parental concern and involvement and social activism which insists on a responsible administration, professional and committed teachers, continuing faculty and staff development, safe, pleasant and encouraging and fully-equipped campuses and an inclusive and culture-respecting curriculum which stresses mastery of knowledge as well as critical thinking, academic excellence, social responsibility, and an expanded sense of human possibility. This was agreed to in consensus then, and must continue to advocate and struggle for now.

4. Economic Development

We will establish a Black Economic Development Fund, with the support of millions, to aid in building an economic infrastructure. We will also offer housing ownership opportunities to check the adverse tide of gentrification. The Millions More Movement will produce and distribute its own products and support "Buy Black" campaigns.

5. Political Power

The Millions More Movement is the political voice of the poor and disenfranchised. We are resolved to take an independent political path in order to achieve political power. The Millions More Movement will be an organized political force of consequence in America and all over the world.

6. Reparations

We demand full and complete reparations for the descendants of enslaved Africans. We demand that America take the appropriate steps to help repair the damage done from 300 years of slavery, 100 years of segregation, and fifty years of the misuse and abuse of governmental power to destroy Black organizations and leaders.

7. Prison Industrial Complex

We demand freedom for all political prisoners held in US prisons and detention facilities, both foreign and domestic. We demand an end to police brutality, mob attacks, racial profiling, the herding of our young men and women into prisons, and the biological and chemical warfare perpetrated against our people.

8. Health

We demand an end to the lack of adequate health care in our community and we demand free health care for the descendants of enslaved Africans in this nation. The Millions More Movement will present a Preventive Health Care Plan to our people that will begin with a campaign to educate our people on healthy diets, eating, and exercise habits

9. Artistic/ Cultural Development

We demand a greater accountability and responsibility of our artists, entertainers, industry personnel, and executives, for them to commit to the redevelopment and upliftment of our people. We demand an end to the exploitation of our talent by outside forces. We will make strides in obtaining greater control over the means of production and distribution of our immense artistic talent and creative genius. We advocate for cultural development, and for the knowledge of our original culture to be used as a model for future advancement.

10. Peace

We call for the establishment of peace in the world. We demand an end to wars of foreign aggression waged by the United States Government against other sovereign nations and people. We demand an end to senseless violence and advocate peace amongst street organizations (gangs) and youth.

A Short History of MARCH
The Local Organization in the Twin Cities

In January 1994, several Brothers including Spike Moss, Keith Ellison, Tyrone Terrill, and James Muhammad met in Randy Staten's office to discuss two important items: 1) A federal grand jury had indicted Qubilah Shabazz, the daughter of the late Malcolm X (El-Hajj Malik El-Shabazz). She was charged with using the telephone and traveling interstate to hire a hitman to murder Minister Louis Farrakhan. The group of men felt that Shabazz was set up and believed they needed to support her. 2) The men also came together to organize Black men to attend the Million Man March in Washington DC on October 16, 1995. The Nation of Islam and the Honorable Minister Louis Farrakhan were lead in organizing this amazing March. The purpose was for Black men to take responsibility for their own actions, to help develop their own communities, and to atone for their lack of responsibility. The local organizing group chartered buses and vans to take hundreds of men to DC.

After the March, the men of MARCH continued to meet every Saturday at Harvest Preparatory School to organize around the principles of

community development. They became a 501c3 non-profit organization. MARCH had a serious educational component that every man had to take before becoming a member. This political educational process was called the Institute for Cultural and Political Change. The core areas of lecture and discussion were: (1) History; (2) Culture; (3) Law and Politics; and (4) Race, Racism, and White supremacy. MARCH had a rites of passage program for boys called Junior March. Tyrone Terrell often stated that MARCH was the greatest volunteer program in the Twin Cities. Furthermore, this local organizing group of the Million Man March may be the last one in existence from the hundreds that were started in 1995.

Men of MARCH

<u>Partial List of MARCH members:</u>

Terrell Akons, Alfred Babington-Johnson, *James Beard*, Daniel Bergin, Andre Bullock, *Eric Coleman*, Lester Collins, *David Cook*, Sam Cooke, *Kelly Day*, *George de Clouet*, Mahmoud El-Kati, Keith Ellison, Bill English, Akil Foluke, Alemu Foluke, *Loyace Foreman III*, *Emmit "Corky" Galloway*, Curtis Harmon, Eric Harmon, Peter Hayden, *John James*, *Garret Johnson Sr.*, *DJ Jones*, Nambago Kalema, *Kamau Kambui*, Nathaniel Khaliq, Rev. Jerry McAfee, Fancy Ray McCloney, Al McFarlane, *William "Billy" McGee*, Resmaa Menakem, Yusef Mgeni, *Meredith "Butch" Miller*, Rev. Devin Miller, Spike Moss, Min. James Muhammad, *Paul Norman*, *Paul Ratliff*, *Thomas "Muata" Ross*, *Elizabeth "Liz" Samuels* (Honorary member), James Sanderson, *William "Bill" Smith*, Marvin Smith, *Randolph Staten*, Leon Tazel, Phillip Terrill, Tyrone Terrill, Shay Whitaker

This is not an exhaustive list of members and my apologies to the Brothers of MARCH that I may have left off of this list. It was not intentional, but was a lack of memory. The Brothers of MARCH in *italics* have transitioned into ancestorhood and I honor them and their work. Thank you, Brothers!

Photos

Million Man March
Washington DC

On Monday, October 16, 1995 there was a sea of Black men, many who stood for 10 hours or more sharing, learning, listening, fasting, hugging, crying, laughing, and praying. The day produced a spirit of brotherhood, love, and unity like never before experienced among Black men in America. All creeds and classes were present: Christians, Muslims, Hebrews, Agnostics, nationalists, pan-Africanists, civil rights organizations, fraternal organizations, rich, poor, celebrities, and people from nearly every organization, profession, and walk of life were present. It was a day of atonement, reconciliation, and responsibility.

Million Man March - Washington DC:
Library of Congress, Washington, D.C.
(reproduction no. LC-DIG-ppmsca-38892)

Some of the founding members of MARCH, circa 1994:

Left to right: Randolph Staten, Al McFarlane, Minister James Muhammad, Peter Hayden, Mahmoud El-Kati, Tyrone Terrill, Bill English, Marvin Smith, Keith Ellison, Leon Tazel, Spike Moss, *unknown,* and Reverend Devin Miller.

Photo by Gene McMillen.

MARCH members, circa 2011:

Left to Right: Nambago Kalema, Thomas Muata Ross, Milford Johnson, Tyrone Terrill, Alemu Foluke, and Elijah Jackson.

MARCH members, circa 2015

Left to Right: Alemu Foluke, Chris Simmons, Tyrone Terrill, Fancy Ray McCloney, Milford Johnson, Nathaniel Khaliq, Hosea, Sam Cooke, and Eddie Cotton

MARCH Members and Community Members
circa 2022

Left to right: Akil Foluke, Donnie Brooks, Alemu Foluke, Kay G. Wilson, Spike Moss, Sam Cooke, Jerome Hamilton Jr., William Moore, Tyrone Terrill, Jerome Hamilton Sr., Elijah Jackson, Ken Rance Jr., Milford

Johnson, Nathaniel Khaliq, Lester Collins, Machi, Leon Tazle, Walter Q. "Bear" Banks, Robert Dixon, and Ken Rance Sr.

MARCH members, circa 1999:

Front row: Christian and Louise. Middle row: Alfred Sanders Jr., Akil Foluke, Iman, Tristian Jaycox, unkown, and Alexander Robinson. Back Row: Cedric Hughes, Thomas Muata Ross, Antonio Robinson, Romero Green, and Milford Johnson.

Milford Johnson and Phillip Terrill at Golden
Thyme Coffeeshop, circa 2017.

Milford Johnson, Tyrone Terrill, and
Fancy Ray McCloney, circa 2017.

Thomas Muata Ross and Milford Johnson, circa 2010.

Phillip Terrill and Akil Foluke circa 2015.

Phillip Terrill, Milford Johnson, and Alemu Foluke –
Wichita, Kansas - September 2022.

Nambago Kalema, Milford Johnson, and Akil
Foluke – Wichita, Kansas - September 2022.

60 Inspiring Quotes to Live By

Each week on KMOJ Radio, I would recite and read quotes to inspire our community. These quotes come from various sources and many come from members of the Black community. Our wisdom is deep and wide. Hotep.

1

"In life if you win, say nothing. If you lose, say less."

- Paul Brown

2

"Our biggest expense is knowledge. Ignorance is free."

- Unknown

3

"In youth we learn; in age we understand."

- Marie von Ebner-Eschenbach

4

"Tough times never last, but tough people do!"

- Robert H. Schuller

5

"The most common way people give up their power is by thinking they don't have any."

- Alice Walker

6

"If you want to be seen, stand up. If you want to be heard, speak up. If you want to be appreciated, shut up."

- Bill Cosby

7

"Not his friends nor his enemies drove him to his evil ways."

- Unknown

8

"You can't wear a crown with your head down."

- Beyonce, Black is King, 2020.

9

"Imagination is more important than knowledge."

- Albert Einstein

10

"Only you have the ability to do the right thing."

- Unknown

11

"The most important thing a father can do for his children is to love their mother."

- Theodore Hesburgh

12

"It only takes a moment to make a moment."

- Anthony Signorelli

13

Let me give you a word of the philosophy of reforms. The whole history of the progress of human liberty shows that all concessions yet made to her august claims have been born of earnest struggle. . .

If there is no struggle, there is no progress. Those who profess to favor freedom and yet deprecate agitation are men who want crops

without plowing the ground. They want rain without thunder and lightning. They want the ocean without the roar of its mighty waters.

The struggle may be a moral one or it may be a physical one, or it may both moral and physical, but it must be a struggle. Power concedes nothing without a demand. It never has and it never will. Find out just what a people will submit to, and you have found out the exact amount of injustice and wrong which will be imposed upon them; and these will continue till they are resisted with either words or blows, or with both. The limits of tyrants are prescribed by the endurance of those whom they oppress.

In the light of these ideas, Negroes will be hunted in the North, and held and flogged in the South so long as they submit to those devilish outrages, and make no resistance, either moral or physical.

Men may not get all they pay for in this world, but they must certainly pay for all they get. If we ever get free from the oppression and wrongs heaped upon us, we must pay for their removal. We must do this by labor, by

suffering, by sacrifice, and, if needs be, by our lives and the lives of others.

- Frederick Douglass
"West India Emancipation" speech, August 4, 1857.

14

What, to the American slave, is your 4th of July? I answer: a day that reveals to him, more than all other days in the year, the gross injustice and cruelty to which he is the constant victim. To him, your celebration is a sham; your boasted liberty, an unholy license; your national greatness, swelling vanity; your sounds of rejoicing are empty and heartless; your denunciations of tyrants, brass fronted impudence; your shouts of liberty and equality, hollow mockery; your prayers and hymns, your sermons and thanksgivings, with all your religious parade, and solemnity, are, to him, mere bombast, fraud, deception, impiety, and hypocrisy — a thin veil to cover up crimes which would disgrace a nation of savages.

- Frederick Douglass
*"What to a Slave is the 4th of July?" speech,
July 5, 1852.*

15

Where justice is denied, where poverty is enforced, where ignorance prevails, and where any one class is made to feel that society is an organized conspiracy to oppress, rob and degrade them, neither persons nor property will be safe.

- Frederick Douglass
Speech on twenty-fourth anniversary of the Emancipation Proclamation, September 22,1886.

16

"I prayed for twenty years but received no answer until I prayed with my legs."

- Frederick Douglass

17

"It is easier to build strong children than to repair broken men."

- Frederick Douglass

18

I am for any movement where there is a just cause to promote, a right to be asserted, a chain to be broken, a burden to be lifted, and a wrong to be redressed. In the struggle for Social Justice, the only reward is to be in the struggle.

- Frederick Douglass

19

"Education is our passport to the future, for tomorrow belongs to the people who prepare for it today."

- Malcolm X

20

I've had enough of someone else's propaganda....I'm for truth, no matter who tells it. I'm for justice, no matter who it is for or against. I'm a human being first and foremost, and as such I'm for whoever and whatever benefits humanity as a whole.

- Malcolm X
The Autobiography of Malcom X

21

There is nothing in our book, the Koran, that teaches us to suffer peacefully. Our religion teaches us to be intelligent. Be peaceful, be courteous, obey the law, respect everyone; but if someone puts his hand on you, send him to the cemetery.

- Malcolm X
"Message to the Grass Roots" speech,
November 10, 1963, Detroit, MI.

22

Of all our studies, history is best qualified to reward our research. And when you see that you've got problems, all you have to do is examine the historic method used all over the world by others who have problems similar to yours. And once you see how they got theirs straight, then you know how you can get yours straight.

- Malcolm X
"Message to the Grass Roots" speech,
November 10, 1963, Detroit, MI

23

"We will work with anybody, anywhere, at any time, who is genuinely interested in tackling the problem head-on."

- Malcolm X
"The Ballot or the Bullet" speech
April 3, 1964, Cleveland, OH

24

When you control a man's thinking you do not have to worry about his actions. You do not have to tell him not to stand here or go yonder. He will find his 'proper place' and will stay in it. You do not need to send him to the back door. He will go without being told. In fact, if there is no back door, he will cut one for his special benefit. His education makes it necessary.

- Dr. Carter G. Woodson
The Mis-Education of the Negro

25

"The most dangerous creation of any society is the man who has nothing to lose."

- James Baldwin
The Fire Next Time

26

I leave you a thirst for education. Knowledge is the prime need of the hour. More and more, Negroes are taking full advantage of hard-won opportunities for learning, and the educational level of the Negro population is at its highest point in history. We are making greater use of the rights and privileges inherent in living a democracy. If we continue in this trend, we will be able to rear increasing numbers of strong, purposeful men and women, equipped with vision, mental clarity, health, and education.

- Mary McLeod Bethune
My Last Will and Testament

27

"The cause of freedom is not the cause of a race or a sect, a party or a class, – it is the cause of human kind, the very birthright of humanity."

- Anna Julia Cooper
A Voice from the South

28

"You are not and yet you are; your thoughts, your deeds and, above all, your dreams."

- W. E. B. Du Bois
The Autobiography of W. E. B. Du Bois

29

"The slave went free; stood a brief moment in the sun; then moved back again toward slavery."

- W. E. B. Du Bois
Black Reconstruction in America

30

"Children learn more from what you are, than what you teach."

- W. E. B. Du Bois

31

Now is the accepted time, not tomorrow, not some more convenient season. It is today that our best work can be done and not some future day or future year.

- W. E. B. Du Bois

32

"Believe in life! Always human beings will progress to greater, broader, and fuller life."

- W. E. B. Du Bois

33

"Either the United States will destroy ignorance or ignorance will destroy the United States."

- W. E. B. Du Bois
*"Niagara Movement" speech,*1905.

34

One ever feels his two-ness, – an American, a Negro; two souls, two thoughts, two unreconciled strivings; two warring ideals in one dark body, whose dogged strength alone keeps it from being torn asunder.

- W. E. B. Du Bois
The Souls of Black Folk

35

"If the truth is told, the youth can grow."

- Nas
I Can lyrics, 2003

36

"I know I can be what I wanna be, if I work hard at it, I'll be where I wanna be."

– Nas
I Can lyrics, 2003

37

"You better check yo' self before you wreck yo' self."

> \- Ice Cube
> *Check Yo Self lyrics,* 2010.

38

"Rappers spit rhymes that are mostly illegal, MCs spit rhymes to uplift their people."

> \- KRS-One
> *MC's Lyrics*

39

"We can't change the world unless we change ourselves."

> \- Biggie Smalls "The Notorious B.I.G."

40

"Live your life, live it right. Be different, do different things."

> \- Kendrick Lamar
> *Kush & Corinthians lyrics,* 2011

41

"When you undervalue what you do, the world will undervalue who you are."

- Oprah

42

"Turn your wounds into wisdom."

- Oprah

43

"True peace is not merely the absence of tension; it is the presence of justice."

- Martin Luther King Jr
Stride Toward Freedom

44

The ultimate measure of a man is not where he stands in moments of comfort and convenience, but where he stands at times of challenge and controversy.

- Martin Luther King Jr
Strength to Love

45

Injustice anywhere is a threat to justice everywhere. We are caught in an inescapable network of mutuality, tied in a single garment of destiny. Whatever affects one directly, affects all indirectly.

- Martin Luther King Jr
Letter from Birmingham, Alabama jail

46

Everybody can be great…because anybody can serve. You don't have to have a college degree to serve. You don't have to make your subject and verb agree to serve. You only need a heart full of grace. A soul generated by love.

- Martin Luther King Jr
"The Drum Major Instinct" speech,
February 4, 1968, Atlanta, GA

47

Education must enable one to sift and weigh evidence, to discern the true from the false, the

real from the unreal, and the facts from the fiction. The function of education, therefore, is to teach one to think intensively and to think critically.

- Dr. Martin Luther King Jr
The Purpose of Education

48

Change will not come if we wait for some other person or if we wait for some other time. We are the ones we've been waiting for. We are the change that we seek.

- Barack Obama

49

"A change is brought about because ordinary people do extraordinary things."

- Barack Obama

50

"Time is a gift you give to other people."

- Michelle Obama

51

"Don't go down a road that you can't come back on."

- Milford's mother, Alice Johnson

52

"Don't let someone else create your world for you, for when they do, they will make it too small."

- Edwin Cole

53

"I've learned that people will forget what you said, people will forget what you did, but people will never forget how you made them feel."

- Maya Angelou

54

"Education is the most powerful weapon which you can use to change the world."

- Nelson Mandela
Speech, June 23, 1990

55

"There is no greater agony than bearing an untold story inside you."

- Maya Angelou

56

"If I am not for myself, who will be for me? But if I am for my own self, what am I? And if not now, when?"

- Rabbi Hillel

57

"Luck is what happens when preparation meets opportunity."

- Seneca

58

"The two most important days of your life are the day you were born and the day you find out why."

- Mark Twain

59

"If you don't understand white supremacy, then everything else that you think you understand will only confuse you."

- Neely Fuller Jr.

60

"A lie doesn't become truth, wrong doesn't become right and evil doesn't become good just because it's accepted by a majority."

- Booker T. Washington

Index of Quotes